UNLEASHED POTENTIAL

Simple Steps to Be The Best Version of Yourself

JEFF FORRESTER

ACITVE FUTURES, LLC

Printed in the United States of America

First Printing, 2020

ISBN 978-0-578-70337-4 (Print)

ISBN 978-0-578-70339-8 (Ebook)

Active Futures, LLC

For bulk orders: 4activefutures@gmail.com

CONTENTS

FOREWORD

It's been my longstanding belief that the greatest teacher in life is experience. Good old fashioned trial and error. Now there are two ways to look at that. The first is the most common, your experience and what you can take away from it. The second, or other option, is learning from somebody else's experience.

When it comes to the first, there is no substitute for going through it alone. Sometimes you just have to learn wisdom by living life. But when it comes to the latter, well, why not avoid some pitfalls or gain advantage of wisdom by modeling somebody who has been there before, maybe even experienced something similar to what you're going through?

When I seek the second type of experience, I don't trust that to just anybody. There's a lot of information out there and the resources to choose from are abundant. But personally, for me, I do my homework. If I'm going to give somebody my valuable time and invest in what they have to teach, I'm going to make sure they are three things;

1. Trustworthy and knowledgeable
2. Not only talk the talk, but walk the walk
3. In it for the right reasons

Jeff checks off all of these boxes for me. In this book you will quickly discover his teaching comes through the vulnerability of his story. No sugar-coating or rah-rah stuff, just real life experience.

He's sincere and passionate in wanting to make a difference in the way we see ourselves and what we may perceive as limitations to our own success or happiness.

His lessons on facing adversity, hard work, resilience, self esteem, faith and being intentional are ones which anybody can relate to and benefit from.

That being said, this book aside, let me tell you from my heart a little bit about the man whose words you're about to read. You see, I've been around the block a time or two, and I've seen a lot of what this world has to offer in terms of teaching and self development.

And to be honest, most of it I wouldn't give a second look to.

And in all transparency, if you asked my wife what is perhaps my greatest liability and yet my greatest quality she'd say "you don't have the ability to fake a compliment."

Guilty as charged. So when I tell you that the author of this book, Jeff Forrester, is one of the most sincere, well respected and unselfish people I've ever met, you can take it to the bank. He's somebody who I strive to emulate and who makes me want to be a better man.

And finally, and most important, is that last box I mentioned checking off. Jeff's heart is in the right place. There's no doubt in my mind he had you, the reader, front and center, as he wrote every word.

This man will love on you though his words and inspire you with his stories, which makes me excited for you, because you're going to put this book down after reading it knowing that you've been better equipped with tools to achieve your goals in this life and you'll possess a greater capacity to know carry out and live up to your greatest potential.

David Norrie

Host, TurnedOn Podcast, author of the best-selling book, Turned On: Tuning In, In a Tuned-Out World

www.TurnedOn.com

WHO AM I?

By most standards, my childhood was normal. During the 70s, I lived at home with my brother, mom, and dad. It was a small house with three bedrooms and one bathroom, but it was home to our family. My parents were hard-working Christian people and there is no doubt they loved my brother and me very much. My dad, Bill, owned a toy store when my brother and I were growing up. I bet you just said to yourself, "that would be so awesome growing up with a dad who owned a toy store!" Well, it was, but not in the way you probably think. He gave me the employee discount of 25% off any regular priced toy I wanted, and occasionally, at cost! I'm not joking! But there's a lesson here. It's a lesson he was teaching me, and one I believe to be important to this day. What's the lesson? Nothing is free. There must be a proper exchange, and you are required to earn what you desire in most cases. If you want it, work for it. Dad certainly did that. He worked harder than anyone I know. Most of my childhood he worked six days a week and most of them were 9 AM to 9 PM Monday through Friday and 9 AM to 6 PM on Saturday. Many days we would take him dinner prepared by my mom and it was the highlight of my day because I got to see him.

Now, my dad had this way about him that most everyone loved. He was a jokester and made people laugh; it was always a joy to be around dad. Early in my childhood, dad's toy store, named Toyland, was very successful. He opened a second store in an up and coming retail area of our small town, but that didn't work out so well for him financially. I don't have a lot of memories of this second store, but I know it didn't stay open very long. One thing I know is it caused him and my mom a lot of stress, and I don't think he ever overcame it. Dad was good about hiding any signs of stress from my brother and me, and, in fact, I never saw the stress manifest in any other way than exhaustion when he came home. He just wanted to drink his tea, smoke his cigarette, and watch TV.

I didn't see dad very much when I was growing up. Most of the time I was already in bed when he came home. He had strong, hardworking values he instilled in me and we will get into those a little later. As time went on, national competition came into town and squeezed the small business owner out, transitioning the business over to a hobby business. He sold R/C planes, cars, model rockets, plastic models, and other items like that. Initially, this was an excellent move for him because there weren't any other stores like this in our little town of Gainesville, but it quickly sputtered a bit and he was growing exhausted from chasing bills and being chained to the business so much. Then in 1990, he got sick. He had what everyone thought was a persistent case of walking pneumonia. It kept getting worse when my mom finally put her foot down and made him go to the doctor. Remember before when I shared that he liked his cigarettes? The symptoms he had been experiencing for months turned out to be related to stage four lung cancer that had metastasized to his brain and other organs. Doctors diagnosed him on the Wednesday before Thanksgiving 1990. I remember being scared, but I was so naïve I really didn't know what we, as a family, were up against. They admitted him immediately and started chemotherapy. Dad's biggest concern was how this would affect us. To this day, I am amazed at how unselfish he was, even when he was staring death in the eye.

Cancer treatment was brutal on dad's body. He was hospitalized every time, and finally, after three rounds, they stopped. It was just too toxic for his body. Three key moments jump out to me through this part of my life. First, after being diagnosed dad went forward at church to ask for forgiveness for his sin of smoking. He was confident this caused his illness. I never saw him play the victim card. Second to that was the power of his mind and will. He told my mom he wanted to live long enough to see me graduate from high school, and he did. He died almost one month to the day later, on July 5, 1991. Last, the day before he died he couldn't open his eyes and speak but he mustered the strength to say, "Don't let her spend any money." You read that right. The last statement was a true testament to my dad's nature. He was a simple man and knew he hadn't left her much insurance money. I wish I could tell you it was something out of a movie, but it wasn't. He shaped my life and while he was sick, he shared with my mother how he wished he had spent more time with my brother and me and taught us the skills he had. I will never forget this and the impact he had on me positively and negatively (more to that later). I know my Dad loved me with everything that he had. I was his buddy!

My mother is an amazing woman, and she has

always been amazing. She was a stay at home mom and assisted my dad with the store once it transitioned over to Hobbyland. My mom was the CEO of our home. She worked tirelessly to clean up after 3 boys (me, my brother, and my dad). She is a bit of a neat freak and that is where I get it from. My mom is so strong and positive. Growing up, I saw her take wonderful care of my dad while he was healthy and then when he was sick. She never complains, always has a smile on her face, is so unselfish, and thinks the best of everyone she meets. I marveled at how positive she always was and is. Mom and dad got into multi-level marketing that was so popular in the 80s and she became obsessed with positive thinking and self-help. She had cassettes of the great motivational speakers of the time and I would listen to them all the time. An elementary-age child listening to self-help motivational tapes isn't normal, but I know this has made me into who I am today. Mom encouraged it and would sing to us, "Think positive, believe you can do anything that you plan, if you will life will treat you grand. Think positive, man." It brings an enormous smile to my face to reflect on that. How cool is it to have a mom who is so positive? It's very cool. I would say I was an "unfocused" student and anything that was difficult I just wouldn't do, so here comes the mom calvary! She is the only reason I think I survived primary school. She would call out spelling words and help me with projects. She was relentless, but very loving throughout the entire time. Some of this, I feel, enables me to give up more quickly than most because I was not used to being challenged and pushed in hard times. More on that later.

After my dad's diagnosis, that is when she put on her cape and showed us she was a superhero. She sacrificed everything for the next 8 months to take care of my dad. She did everything and I am sure she was physically and emotionally exhausted but never showed it. She was and is a pillar of strength few humans possess. I kept the doors open to the store and she would manage the books and the bills all while taking care of my dad. I really don't know how she did it. I love her so much and am so thankful God blessed this earth with her.

Then, there is my brother, Will. I won't go too much into our relationship as kids because it was the normal brothers four years apart and nothing in common. We played a ton together in our small neighborhood because there weren't many other kids. He and I are much closer now and enjoy spending time together and even talking business. Will has been in the fashion merchandising business for over 25 year. I learn something from Will every time we speak, especially about business as he is highly skilled and knowledgeable about all aspects of the business. I have always looked up to him because he has always voiced his feelings much better than me. Now sometimes I wish he wouldn't voice them all, but it is something I should work on. We all have our strengths, right? I love my brother a ton and he means a lot to me. I won't go too much into our relationship because this isn't a life story about me and him.

Since you have read a bit about my immediate family, it's time to go into my childhood a bit. As a child, I struggled with self-esteem and self-image as I grew older. I was a funny, sensitive kid but wasn't an extroverted kid. I recall being terrified to speak to strangers and anyone I wasn't very familiar with. I was afraid. I know many kids are like this, but this has stuck with me most of my life. I wasn't and am still not the life of the party because I was and am concerned with how others think about me. I love the comfort of the familiar. I never liked to spend the night away from home because it was different and scary, and I just didn't like it. I would have, but I wasn't an adventure seeker, so I missed out on a lot of stuff just because I feared trying and failing. I was the definition of a fixed mindset. I became good at making excuses and lies why I wouldn't or couldn't do something that scared me. I avoided anything difficult and slowly felt like I was weird. This thinking stuck with me for a very long time, deep into my adult life. I wanted things easy. I expected things to be easy.

I talked to myself in my head a lot as a kid. I mean a lot. Not in a multiple personality way, at least I don't think so, but I had dialogue where I would talk myself out of things and then beat myself up after for being afraid. Looking back, I wonder why I did that since I listened to so many self-help and positivity tapes? I had a happy childhood. I was just limited with the self-imposed fear I had. Like a lot of kids, I was "husky" once I hit 4th grade, and I stayed that way until I was in college. It started out as genetics and then grew into just eating way too many ice cream sandwiches and bacon double cheeseburgers! I loved to eat. It tasted good, and it made me feel great. I had a very unhealthy relationship with food. Feel bad, eat. Feel good, eat. I had no governor on when it was too much. Being overweight as a child is a magnet to getting picked on by everyone. I hated my body and how I looked but was unwilling to put in the work to change it. I remember praying that I would go to sleep and then wake up looking like one of the professional wrestlers on TV. People are cruel, and I didn't handle it well. I drew further into my shell or hid it with picking on other people or being a class clown. Words are powerful, and I believed what people would say. This feeling began the vicious cycle of my need to be accepted; I needed it, I desired it.

I loved movies! They allowed me to escape reality and dream of being an adventurer in space or the desert. I could finally be the hero everyone admired and looked up to. My dad sold role-playing games at the store and late in elementary and early middle school I met some other boys who enjoyed the imagination of an adventure just like I did. This holds very fond memories for me. Many people would consider us "geeks" or nerds because we weren't the jocks everyone thought you had to be, but we spent hours developing the skills of our characters, eating junk food and laughing hysterically when something crazy happened. It was marvelous! I continued to play well into my college years, but not as much as before. There were many nights spent sitting around a kitchen table rolling dice. Don't knock it until you've tried it.

I found sports in the 8th grade and fell in love with basketball. It was a team of my friends because I went to a small Christian school so there weren't many to pick from and I am happy about that because otherwise, I would have never found sports. I had attempted on two different occasions to go to larger schools to play football because of my size but as I mentioned earlier; I didn't enjoy pushing myself or doing anything difficult, so I quit there too.

After graduating high school, I started on the path of losing the excess weight and connected with a couple of friends who wanted to go to the gym. I loved it. Lifting and getting stronger gave me an identity and purpose. This was the first time I enjoyed working hard because someone pushed me past what I thought I could do. The weight came off, and I lost 20lbs in the first month. This was great; I was still overweight, but now I'm strong and so I had delusions that I was far more talented than I was. I lived in a strange fantasy world I had created that gave me some peace because it was all talk. I never had to deliver. Over the next several years I would learn more about weight loss and kicked it in. I just knew if I could lose weight the ladies would like me. I worked hard on losing the weight through eating better and riding my bike everywhere. I ended up losing 85lbs! That's an amazing accomplishment, right? I'm proud of what I did, but not that proud of why I did it. I lost the weight in the hopes other people would accept me, and I would accept me. The issue was people accepted me at my heaviest, but I was the one who got in the way.

I worked throughout my college years. I wasn't an exceptional student in high school and I am very thankful for Santa Fe Community College and the teachers there. They saved my academic career. I needed to take remedial classes because I skipped the SAT out of fear. Do you see a trend? I finally performed to a standard that afforded me the chance to get into the College of Journalism and Communications at the University of Florida. It thrilled me! My generation was expected to graduate from college and now I had the opportunity to obtain an undergraduate degree in public relations. I loved public relations and learning about marketing, public speaking, and journalism. The classes were interesting and I could listen in class and do well on the tests because most of the classes weren't necessarily focused on tests, but projects. I'm very task-oriented and can nail projects and lead a group well. I was diligent and worked hard to graduate in two years after I started. I'm now a college graduate from the University of Florida. I never thought that would happen. So much so, I asked President Lombardi when I accepted my diploma if I could give him a hug!

Now it is time to get a "real" job. My mom and I had struggled financially for the last couple of years and we both discussed how my Dad had grown tired of owning his own business and didn't see that he had other options, so we both thought it best to be someone else's employee with good benefits and a steady paycheck. I really enjoyed running the family business. I learned so much from the day-to-day operations and the lessons my dad had taught my mom and me that are still with me today. I learned creativity and how to sell. These two things landed me my first job.

My roommate at the time was part owner in the family business of selling technology to the education market. He invited me to go help him on an installation for a couple of weeks and after showing how I could perform they offered me a sales job. I was so excited. I'll never forget and can see it like it just happened. It's my first day as a salesman, and I have my golf shirt and khakis on. I sat down at the desk they assigned me and my roommate's boss walked up with the Florida directory of schools and a how-to networking book, flopped them down on the desk, and said: "Go get em!" There I am with zero real computer skills expected to sell computers and wireless networking to schools. Cold calling schools! My roommate and his family were bootstrap kind of people. Self-made and successful, and why wouldn't I be the same. The part of me ruled by fear wished they would have held my hand and gave me everything. But, the grateful, more mature me is grateful they managed me the way they did. I didn't dig as much as I should have, but I was a sponge listening to the techs in the back. I learned the lingo. Shared chocolate chip cookies and lunch with these guys, and it helped.

This started me knowing the importance of not depending on other people to help me. How badly did I want to be successful? I wanted it and needed to put the work in, but still whined and complained on many occasions and had a victim mentality. I could have done so much more there, but I had an awesome opportunity presented to me in 1999 to get into pharmaceutical sales. It terrified me. I wasn't good at science. I avoided it, but here I am facing my fears. I had some good friends and great trainers who gave me confidence that I didn't need to know it all and they would teach me what I needed to know. Fortunately, I met my best friend still to this day, and he was a biology major. Thanks, Butch! I passed the initial pass-fail test. This was old school pharma where you went to training and if you didn't pass they sent you back to your room and you flew home without a job! This rocked my anxiety and worry. I always went to the worst-case scenario versus being confident in my intelligence. Turns out I'm an intelligent guy. This was the beginning of the next 21 years of my professional career. During my career, I have had the fortune of learning from different people and holding a variety of positions. I have been in customer-facing sales, training, marketing, and leadership. I established a new passion for learning and improving by consuming as much self-development material as possible. In each role, I committed to learning skills that would elevate my skills and performance and wasn't dependent on other people to help me. Remember my first job out of college and the book flopped on the desk? Other than basic product knowledge, these billion-dollar pharmaceutical companies and leaders do the same thing. I learned that no one cares about your development as much as you do. I agree and disagree with that statement. I thought no one cared as much for their development as I did. When I was in training and leadership most people I worked with showed little interest in getting better. Now they said they were, but most weren't willing to make the commitment to put in the work or put the ego aside to hear other people's ideas. I struggled with this and with my low self-esteem. I took it as I was failing and then masked that with arrogant humility that my way was the best. I was moving up the ladder so why wouldn't they want to do it my way. I mean they weren't taking any initiative so at least my way would get them further right? I look back and shake my head at myself. I wanted them to be successful and reach new heights, but I was doing it so I would get the credit. That's awful. I should have wanted them to be successful for them, not only myself.

With time and reflection, I have seen the importance of being intentional in everything we do. Nothing worthwhile happens by chance. We must make it happen. We should be active in our own development in every aspect of our lives. Take me, for example. I was active and intentional in my professional career, but winging it with my faith and my family. What was I thinking? If I want to be the best man I can be, I need to be intentional, in each aspect of my life and so do you. I believe you should identify your strengths and your weaknesses foremost and then go to work! Ask for help. Share these things with people in your circle of influence. Doing this has changed my life! I'm serious and this isn't just a line to sell the book. I am a different man than I was two years ago and I like me for once in my life.

I'm still a work in progress, but once I committed to aligning my life properly with faith first, family second, and work third all three are doing great!

My goal is for you to see where I came from and learn the four key things I have learned and coached 100s of people in the past 21 years that can take you from being just ordinary with your faith, family, and professional career. Keep an open mind and commit to holding yourself accountable to put in the work. You must do the work and I am confident when you stop delegating your development you will create the perfect path for you.

GETTING TO KNOW WHO YOU ARE IS IMPORTANT!

Why is understanding who you are so important? While it seems like a simple question to answer, if you dig in, you will discover it is not so cut and dry. We are all unique individuals. In my opinion, everything starts with understanding who you are. Understanding who you are, including your strengths and weaknesses, will not only help you develop, it will help you raise your children better, have a deeper relationship with your spouse/partner, family members, and friends. It will also help you become a better professional. Personal development requires a lifelong commitment because, as we age, we are always learning, and we have an opportunity to grow each day that passes. If we aren't paying attention to this, then we will miss critical opportunities to take advantage of challenges to overcome. Take me, for instance. I know that I suffer from anxiety and obsessive thinking, which can be harmful. Thoughts will get into this brain and spin out of control, and the biggest issue is when it's not a positive, exciting thought. It's the worst-case scenario almost all the time. I have a son that has the same brain! I can see it in his eyes when something gets into his head and starts spinning. He has had this since he was small.

When he was two years old, my wife told him in the summer, maybe July or August, that we were going to Walt Disney world and showed him a picture of the castle, and this started a daily discussion about "castle in January." Anytime something Disney popped up, he talked about it. I know this is a simple example most parents can relate to, but I wanted to provide this as a fun example because there are other similar situations not as fun to share. I realized my obsessive thinking was a weakness. Still, I also overcame it. Considering I was honest with myself and worked to understand the triggers and tips to help me overcome them, I can share these with my son and others. Anyone with these thoughts needs to know you are not abnormal for thinking this way. It is critically important to understand yourself because it will and does impact others. I have also experienced not knowing or just avoiding/ignoring strengths. Ignoring your strengths often isn't the challenge, but it happens. There are dangers in this as well. I have a double whammy of a weakness, pushing me to avoid strength, and this is where the danger lies. As I explained earlier about my childhood, I was an introverted fat kid with a very low self-image and self-esteem, and this created a roadblock for my strengths. I was so concerned with what others would think or say (a weakness) I wasn't willing to share my thoughts on how we should plan and organize a task or goal. Turns out, planning and processing a plan and purpose is one of my strengths, and it went unnoticed and was detrimental to the team or my family. I knew this was the right thing to do or the right path to take; however, my weakness blocked my strength which means I avoided using my strength.

Strengths and weaknesses work together, and neither one should be avoided. We know we have both, but our "humility" keeps us from wanting to brag about our strengths (whether they are or aren't, we think they are) or confess our weakness because we will be judged. Focusing too much on either creates an imbalance and inefficiency. Spending too much time on your strengths can provide some success, but eventually, you will reach a ceiling because your weaknesses cap your potential. Conversely, if you focus too much on your weakness, it establishes a victim mentality, and you will never achieve the potential you are made for. See, they equally cause a problem. I can tell you from personal and professional experience that not being honest about both is dangerous. If you don't believe me, there are tons of history books containing story after story about this same topic.

Let's look back at history and why we probably fear sharing our weaknesses. When I was a child, my parents took my brother and me to church and Sunday school, and I enjoyed hearing the stories in the Old Testament. One most are familiar with, maybe not in detail, but familiar none the less is of Samson and Delilah. Samson was the strongest man alive and was blessed by God from birth. Samson's strength came from his hair, and God told him never to cut it. God chose Samson to lead the Israelites out of bondage from the Philistines. Samson had many stories of where his great feats of strength and violence left the Philistines in awe and fear of him. They tried everything, and finally, they convinced Delilah to annoy him and play on his emotions until he told her. After telling her, she told the others, and they came in, shaved his head, plucked out his eyes, and threw him in prison. Ok, whether you are a Bible believer or not, the moral of this story is to keep your weaknesses a secret so other people won't take advantage of them, right? Take, for instance, political campaigns. They prey on weaknesses and spend millions of dollars exploiting those to make themselves look better. No wonder people are afraid to share their vulnerabilities.

No wonder people allow their weaknesses to fester. Festered weaknesses inhibit full potential and personal growth. For me, it is the fear of judgment. Let's be real; having my eyes plucked out seems almost better than being shunned or being judged. Stop and think about it. How many times have you wanted to share something and didn't because you didn't want others judging you? Think about a deep dark secret that you know others won't agree with or understand, but you battle with the demon by yourself. The shame of disappointing others may be the scariest thing keeping people from sharing a weakness, but in all honesty, you will never take the power away from that until you step up and ask for help. Any little thing that distracts you from being the best you can be is the problem. Our habits are in control, and like someone said, "habits eat willpower for lunch!" So many of us ignore our weaknesses. And take it from me, when you ignore them, they will bring you to your knees when you least expect it.

Don't allow your weaknesses to take your power away from you! Find a safe person or group of people and go to work. Each of you share because either you can all work on the same together, or each of you can help inspire the other. We will get more into some of the ideas on this later. The main thing is that we need to change our narrative and applaud other people's strengths and praise someone for sharing their weaknesses. Strengths and weaknesses need to be shared, leveraged, and improved if we want to see the changes we know are possible.

What are the best ways to do this? Like I said before, we are all different, and our past experiences will play into the best ways to uncover our strengths and weaknesses. Some people can sit down with a piece of paper and list their strengths and weaknesses and, through this, can create an advantageous starting point. If this is you, great; so why did you need to read a book to sit down and do this? Think about that one for a few minutes. I feel I can do this now with reasonable accuracy, but the only reason I can is that I listened to previous discussions about my strengths and weaknesses. I am sure though I have blind spots, I need others' input on if I'm looking to increase my potential even further. I may not have fully acted (I mean being consistent over a long period) on working on my weaknesses before, but I remember what I was told. I'll admit I want to be the best version of who I was created to be, and receiving feedback and coaching is all a part of development. Some of this comes from genuine curiosity. But it also comes from my low self-esteem, self-image, and wanting to be accepted by everyone. When you have this going on, you are constantly beating yourself up for not being perfect. The problem with working on weaknesses due to this is all you are doing is masking one for another. The real gap needing attention is the self-image and self-esteem and not the obvious one, because until you get the root cause addressed, you won't get where you want to be.

Another way is to conduct a formal or informal 360-degree feedback session. Sidenote- for those unfamiliar with what a 360-degree feedback session is, it is where you send out requests to multiple people and anonymously those people answer a series of questions that will provide feedback to you to work on. This is very valuable and very scary. Prepare yourself for this one and get your head right. I'm serious. If you're not in a good, confident, healthy space, you should seek a professional therapist because the hard truth can rock your world. The one word of advice is that this exercise will help you more than it will hurt you. Put your ego aside and understand everything you hear can be worked on if you want to. Gaining outside feedback is helpful because we create an internal dialogue of excuses for our weaknesses and shortcomings, and we also limit being proud of our strengths because we don't want to look like we are bragging. Embrace both without emotion. Approach a 360 with an open mind because it will provide a helpful list of things you can leverage more of and a list of things that have been holding you back. Take off the chains of your weaknesses by taking ownership of them and being intentional on improving them.

If doing a 360-degree feedback session isn't an option for you right now, or you just don't want to do one, there are many different personality assessments like DISC that will objectively share strengths and weaknesses. It is called DISC because personalities can be summarized into four different categories. Dominant, Influencing, Steady, and Compliant are what spells DISC. Every person possesses DISC elements, but there is always a trait that surfaces to the top and sometimes a combination of the others. These create the equation of your personality and some of the strengths and weaknesses most have. Personality types have been around since 400 BC when Empedocles defined them as the elements of earth, wind, fire, and water, and Hippocrates described them as choleric, sanguine, phlegmatic, and melancholy. These evolved into DISC when William Marston redefined them in 1926. Our personality types are shaped by our environment, role models, and heredity. These things play an essential role in who we are. I like personality tests because it is scary how close these tests will nail key traits and offer suggestions. A critical part to remember is to answer these based on the area of life you are focusing on. We all can be different in our professional life versus our home life, so pick one and think of answers as they pertain to that area you have selected.

On top of that, personality tests aren't just fun exercises. They need to be a part of your playbook to unleash your potential. Whenever I have asked people if they have taken one, many say yes and know their place on the wheel, their top letters or colors, and that's where it stops. Don't waste your time and money if you aren't willing to put in the work and recommendations offered. Find someone to help you understand and apply the data. Reading this book won't help by itself. Be intentional about being a better you.

IMPORTANCE OF LEVERAGING YOUR STRENGTHS

Do you know what is so funny about success? It's that if you want to have success, you need to experience success. This means you need momentum, but how do you get momentum? Momentum is defined by the impetus (force that makes something happen or happen more quickly. I had to look it up) gained by a moving object. You can't hope for momentum, you must take action. You must stand up and hold yourself accountable for finding something you can have success with right away, so how do you do that? Look to your strengths first! Your strengths are your strengths for a reason, and they come easy to you, right? This is the first step in creating momentum, and why it is so important to leverage your strengths. Take notice I didn't say lean on them because that is passive, but leverage them.

It was August 1991, and my father had passed away a month earlier and my eating was way out of control. I had "bulked up" to a whopping 270 pounds. I was fortunate to have a 6'2" frame to carry the weight, but who are we kidding I was fat! This was me at my heaviest and I had finally had enough. I had "tried" gimmicks from TV first because I thought I could just wear something that would create heat on my body, the weight would fall off, and I would look like the guy in the ad. Wrong! That was my lazy brain taking over. I knew I needed to put work in and with my fixed mindset, I created so many excuses I wasn't going to do it on my own. I'm going to *pause* the story and ask if you remember when I spoke about the DISC personality profile? Well, I am a high S which is characterized as a team player guy. I'm good in groups because they motivate me and I'm great at motivating others. I'm also a C, which is data-driven. I like charts and checklists and being able to look over and track performance. This is a strength of mine. Ask anyone who knows me. Unpause. I knew I needed a group to help me get motivated and hold me accountable since I couldn't do it on my own and a plan I could follow. I got to work on recruiting my group. The first was the roommate of a former coworker. He was my complete opposite. Long hair, tattoos, drove a black StingRay Corvette and said anything that came to his mind. This is my guy! I knew he wouldn't let me off the hook and he knew some about exercising. The second was a great friend who also was a former coworker and one of my game buddies I mentioned earlier. He was in the same boat as me, so I knew he wouldn't be judgmental and we would motivate each other along the way. We did some research and landed on a plan with supplements, a diet plan, and a workout schedule with a chart! Did I mention I love charts? We dug in and followed that plan to a "T"! My workout regimen was consistently five to six days a week. On Monday, Wednesday, and Friday, I trained my chest and back. On Thursday and Saturday, I trained my legs and staggered these regimens in the following weeks. We were diligent, and the weight started falling off and I was getting stronger. In the first month, I dropped twenty pounds! I was ecstatic at the progress. Finally, I started to gain some momentum. We stayed on track for the 90-day plan and I finished the plan losing a total of thirty pounds. What a huge accomplishment for a kid who needed a win. The problem was that after the 90 days were over, I lost my focus on the eating because I didn't learn anything and just followed directions, but I gained momentum. I continued working out and gained a ton of strength. I didn't really understand it at the time, but I found success whenever I leveraged the strengths I had because they came easy/natural for me. I needed a group of people to cheer for and cheer me on, and I also needed to track my success to keep me on track. Support groups and checklists aren't unique to me, but I utilize them in my processes and training. Some may not be so accepting of support groups and checklists; the mere mention of those two words makes their skin crawl. Another important aspect to leveraging your strengths to create momentum is celebrating the wins. You must do this. Your brain needs it. Your soul needs it. This is where my chart came into play during my initial weight loss, and then when I lost the rest of my weight. Following and setting up a chart came easy to me because I am a visual person and I knew that much, but I didn't know it was essential to my success. I just knew I liked to track everything. I kept marking and writing down the weights I was gaining on my lifts and losing on my body. It was awesome. One was going up and one was coming down and weekly we would all look at our notebook and congratulate one another; these celebrations motivated us to keep going and we did. Seeing the success and tracking it encouraged me to add more weight to the lift the following week and push and be more diligent in eating the right foods. Funny how that works, add more and get stronger; eat better and lose more weight. Do more of the right thing and accomplish more right!

I thought I had it all figured out but didn't realize it wasn't me that had started this momentum, it was my strengths. I started to rely on my workout gang and my chart and why not? These were the formula to success. I was getting stronger and losing weight.

Well, like most relationships in life, these started to fade a bit. Not because of anything bad. They just did. One friend moved out of town and another got a girlfriend. I thought, "now what do I do?" My workout gang was no longer here. Who was going to push me? Tracking goals wasn't fun anymore because I had no one to celebrate with. I had relied on these two and my charts so much I had ignored working on the weaknesses that caused me to be fat. I was relying solely on these two strengths to create momentum which it did, but when a small obstacle presented itself, it mostly came to a screeching halt. Have you encountered a situation like this before? Everything is going great- almost too great and too easy. Strengths are perfect for creating momentum because the wins come quickly, but you can become complacent or even careless because it does come easily; when you least expect it something stops the momentum, you never anticipated. Working out was difficult but by leveraging the natural strengths I had I was able to have success and work through the difficult times. I could do what came naturally and start a process I was comfortable with, and through leveraging those strengths over and over and having the momentum of success I don't need a group to cheer me on. I like it and thrive in it, but I don't need it.

Think about the things you enjoy doing and the things that just seem to come more naturally to you versus other people. Don't limit yourself and don't use logic, yet. Just write everything down you can think of and when you run out of words, then ask a friend or loved one to look it over and add any strength you may have missed. Don't be shy and don't be humble, just write. I am giving you permission to not be humble and brag on yourself. I keep mentioning this because this isn't easy. Most people really struggle with recognizing their value and strengths. If you start to get stuck, reflect on a project or task that you crushed and start to write down the reasons why you were so successful. I bet it was because of some of your outstanding natural strengths. Now is the time to start assigning your strengths to different areas in your life. Some you may already be using, and some you may not have considered it helping in that area. This is fun! You are on a roll. Are you naturally a talker? Do you like to connect like-minded people together? Are you great at organizing? Everyone has strengths that will assist them in unleashing their potential if they are recognized and leveraged! The next step is to identify your top ten strengths, write them on separate post-it notes, and put them somewhere you will see them every day. I put mine around my mirror and I did this to program my brain to know how strong I am and what I need to leverage to get more out of my life. What is fun about this is if you had ten people do this exercise and put them next to one another, no one would have the same ten. Embrace this because great teams accomplish so much more when everyone puts aside ego and allows strengths to be leveraged.

 Doesn't it feel great to see where you can unleash more of your potential by leveraging your strengths where you hadn't considered before? I'll share another personal example that may help paint a better picture. It was 2006, and I received my first promotion of my career. I became a training manager with a small pharmaceutical company. My boss assembled the best team I had ever worked on. Not only did we like each other, but we all had different strengths. The team was tasked to create a training program from the ground up. We had to put together initial training, continual rep training, launch meetings, facilitator's guides, etc. It was a dream come true, and boy did we all learn a lot. We all knew each of us had strengths and were being led to embrace those, and we flourished. We had some creative minds on our team. One guy could come up with some fantastic, big ideas that were fun and would impact the classes we would be training. I'm laughing to myself with some ideas he came up with. I'll just say one whole meeting was centered around a cowbell! No one, and I mean no one, who was at that meeting will ever forget it! Another member of our team was the thinker we desperately needed. No stone would be unturned, and he thought everything through to ensure we had all our bases covered. He would find things we missed or hadn't considered. He also was the smartest of the team. This guy was a product and market place wizard and combined that with a great personality; he wowed any room he was in front of. With all of us young men who would charge after anything, we needed a calming demeanor that would reel us all back a bit. She was more our senior and was the voice of reason to keep us focused on the audience we were working for. We would get excited about our ideas and needed to have someone more level-headed ask some good questions to make sure we had not just thought of a great idea but thought of how others would react. Then there was me. I have always been able to be a jack of all trades. I can blend with each person on the team and help balance each of them to encourage them to do their best. It's funny when I think about it, I have a little of each and a lot of ability to get each unique individual to work as a team. Does that make sense? I could get the creative mind of our team to share his idea to the team and start asking some basic questions that would then get the thinker to start his thorough analysis of it all. As that went on, I would work with the team member who provided us with balance and peace, on gaining her feedback. This enabled us to be able to deliver it to the others so they would be able to process it in their own way. It was a perfect storm of talent and then there was the team leader, he was the conductor of the whole thing. Without his leadership and allowing us to go, it would not have worked. His strength was the lack of ego and a servant leadership mentality. He knew just when to serve up a well-placed question that would have us all pump our breaks or mash down on the accelerator. We accomplished so much. I never worked harder and enjoyed every second of it because we all leveraged our strengths to accomplish our goals.

I share this example to reinforce that by leveraging our strengths we can accomplish so much whether we are on a team or working solo. We were fortunate because it just happened, but imagine if we knew more of who we were and where our strengths could be leveraged more? Where would you fit on that team? Where do you fit on your team professionally, at home, or at your church? You have a lot to offer this world and you need to know so you can raise your hand. Most importantly, use your strength to improve on your weaknesses. Why try to do things the hard way? Once we start considering your weaknesses I will ask you to go back and look at how your strengths will help you.

Let's tie all of you together to unleash your true potential with less effort!

VALUE OF RECOGNIZING A WEAKNESS

I f there was a room of 100 people and they were asked to share their weaknesses, how many do you think would raise their hands? 5%? 10%? Less? How did you feel when you read that? Look, you aren't abnormal or strange if you aren't excited about sharing your weakness. We talked about this earlier that Samson shared his weakness and the next thing that happened was his eyes being plucked out. I like my eyes and would like to keep them! Let's paint a different picture more relevant to what each of us face and look at it from a professional point of view.

It's late February or early March and time for the year-end review with the boss. Maybe having your eyes plucked out sounds better right now. Your boss calls you into their office and starts to discuss the previous year. The pleasantries are flowing and you both are slightly uncomfortable even though it was a great year. You are discussing the things that you do well and both of you are all smiles. You are feeling good about yourself right now. Then your boss' shoulders drop a little bit and their face gets a bit more serious and they ask what could you have done better or for our discussion, your weaknesses. These aren't easy to admit and sometimes difficult to even know. They want to know if you know your weaknesses and either way they are about to tell you, but why are they telling you? Are they telling out of a want to help you get better, are they telling you to make them feel better about themselves, or are they telling you because it's what the form in front of them tells them to. I don't know, but we have all been in that situation and it doesn't matter their motive or sincerity, because a weakness is a weakness even if you don't agree with it. The weakness did hold you back from having an even better year. Don't try to make excuses that it wouldn't have; you know if you would have worked on that a bit more than you did, your year would have ended better than it did.

It is very difficult for most people to see their own weakness because they are too close to it. There are the obvious ones that are easy to admit. There

are ones not so easy to admit, and there are the
ones we don't even see. Why do you think I say
there is value in recognizing your weaknesses?
Why do you need to recognize your weakness?
What is the definition of weakness compared to
strength? I know it seems simple, but why do we
avoid a critical part in unleashing more of our
potential? I won't go into pages and pages of
psychological reasons, but would you care if I did?
There are plenty of books on this subject by people
way more qualified to share that information with
you. I want you to answer these questions yourself.
You should answer these questions yourself. You
need to answer these questions yourself.

I'll let you off the hook on the first question. Why
do I say there is value in recognizing your
weaknesses? I say there is value in it because I did
it. I do it because I have a ton of them and by
working on these weaknesses they aren't nearly as
bad as they used to be. I have improved as a
human simply by admitting I have weaknesses and
openly sharing what those are or were. Can you
say that about yourself? If you can't now, I hope by
the end of this chapter and book you will. I'm
telling you if you don't recognize and work on your
weaknesses, they will hold you back from
unleashing your potential. How can they not? You
can power through most things in life, but if there

is a kink in the armor the enemy will find it eventually. The enemy I am speaking of is the one holding you back from more success.

I have run quite a few half marathons and set goals for myself every year and fallen short most of the time. One time, I didn't train enough, another time my nutrition was off, and most of the time it was both. These are glaring weaknesses I have in my running and accomplishing my goal. I use this as a simple example because if I was to get both my training and nutrition on point I would break my all-time goal of a sub two hours for a half marathon, but since I haven't taken the steps to improve both of them I can't expect to accomplish my goal. I will never accomplish that goal. It's just silly to think otherwise and also I stopped getting mad at myself and beating myself up or feeling sorry for myself when I didn't accomplish the goal (another huge weakness I battle with all the time). Think about this example and how it compares to your professional career or your personal relationships with family and friends. What are the glaring weaknesses you could improve if you wanted to?

Let's put in some fun simple work to start working on those weaknesses and say out loud, "no one is perfect. I am human. I have weaknesses and they won't define me. I have power over my weaknesses!" Seriously, don't just read those words like you just did. Take action and say them out loud. Come on do it! It won't hurt. I know it's scary and you feel embarrassed but it will fill your soul! Before you start to work on your weaknesses you need to take back the power from them. These weaknesses do not define you unless you allow them to. These weaknesses can quickly become a strength and reveal other strengths you didn't even realize you have. I'm not normally an openly rah rah kind of guy, but in overcoming weaknesses I am. I love motivating people to take their power back and build on a growth mindset. If you have read this far in the book you have the mindset to start, and we will work on making sure you build the confidence to take an active role in building the future you want.

Identifying your weaknesses will be like the exercise for identifying strengths. Grab another piece of paper and start writing. I asked you to not be humble for writing down your strengths so I will ask you to not be overly self-critical and beat yourself up for weaknesses- but don't hold back. This list is for you. You took your power back over these and you just are looking for the ones to start crossing off the list. Expose your weaknesses to yourself. This is your chance to show yourself who is boss! This is probably an easier task than writing down your strengths because many of us find it easier to point out our faults/weaknesses versus bragging on ourselves. Once you have exhausted yourself now start to eliminate the words that are similar. Keep doing that until you have it down to ten. These are the ten weaknesses you see that are holding you back. You don't have to have ten and if you don't you may want to add self-awareness as one. Just kidding kind of. If you are like me, you have used these 10 or more as an excuse to let you off the hook for not putting in the work.

What do I mean by an excuse? I'll use another personal story as an example. Growing up I was a fat kid. I told you about that already. I was a fat kid because I ate a lot of unhealthy food and didn't exercise. I also was being programmed with an excuse for my size by other people and I reinforced it. I was convinced that I was just big-boned like most of my family. I allowed my weakness to define me and program me to be unhealthy. I used it as an excuse to not try to get healthy and lose the weight. The excuse was like a warm blanket. If I had one, I wouldn't have to try that hard because I could fall back into its warm embrace. I can't lose weight because I'm naturally that way. False. It's sad how many excuses I made or allowed others to reinforce to justify things in my own head. I finally decided to focus on losing the weight, and I'm not big-boned after all. I have a larger frame, but at one time I got down to 185lbs from 270lbs.

Look at the weaknesses you have written down and ask yourself how many have you been programmed to believe? How many of them do you use as excuses to hold you back from trying something that is scary? These are where your potential is being stifled. These weaknesses are holding you back from unleashing your potential on the world. I know it is scary and you will probably fail along the way in your progress because you may have set your goal for improvement unrealistically, but you will make progress. You will improve. I know you can! This is such an awesome experience because in just writing down your weaknesses you are overcoming a weakness we all possess, and that is a poor self-image. You are taking your power back, I feel it. Pick out one weakness you will work on right now. You can pick any one you want, and I would encourage you to look for the one that won't take the most effort right out of the starting gate. You need wins to build that confidence because if you can improve one of them you can improve all of them. Some will require more work than the others and to me that's the fun part. Take that post-it note with the weakness on it and now put it next to your strengths and find the ones (strengths) you can leverage to improve that weakness. Many people forget this step. You can't. You must identify and use the things that come naturally to help you overcome the things that don't. You have probably done this by chance but now I'm asking you to be intentional about it. When you overcome one you will be riding high!

Think about the accomplishments you are most proud of; these are the ones hardest to achieve. Why are underdog or comeback stories so exciting? They are exciting because we all view ourselves as the underdog and want the storied ending. We want to be seen overcoming the difficult obstacle in our way, but the problem is few want to put in the effort and risk of not coming out on top to put in the work. The work and believing you can overcome is the victory and not the score or the outcome. Are you willing to invest in yourself? Are you willing to go for it on 4th and 11 deep in your own territory? Would you go for it no matter what? Don't wait for life to have your back against the ropes to go for it. The sooner you start to work on improving your weaknesses the more time you will have to correct along the way. Do you want to write yourself off before you even start? I thought about apologizing to you, the reader, for asking so many questions, but I'm not because these are questions you must answer. These are the questions to inspire you to start now. At the time of writing this book, I am 47 years old and some would say I am approaching a challenging age in my professional career. Guys my age should have things figured out. Well, I think I'm just getting started because I'm working on my weaknesses daily with my wife, kids, and a group of accountability partners of all kinds.

I plan on living another 47 years, at least. I'm working on being healthy spiritually, mentally, and physically. I will accomplish a lot more in the next 47 years than I did in the first 47 years. I guarantee it. Can you? Will you? If that doesn't motivate you or connect with you, let me share an example my daughter said while I was sharing this exact story. There is so much wisdom in our children if we just listen, I mean really listen. "Daddy, so if you have a birthday cake and you have eaten half of it and there is still a half left, are you sad there is only a half or are you excited there is still more cake to eat?" What beautiful perspective from a child!

Don't allow the stories you have told yourself to hold you back. Don't allow other people's limiting thoughts and fears to hold you back. Don't ignore your weaknesses. It's very important because take it from me, your weaknesses will rear their head when you least expect it and it will hold you back and many times set you back, but in those setbacks are when I am the clearest. Learn from them and don't allow them to define you or limit you. As I said earlier, there isn't a weakness that you have that cannot be improved upon. None! Put in the work and find your weaknesses to overcome and develop to unleash the potential within you.

WHY DOES IT ALWAYS COME DOWN TO COMMUNICATING?

Why does it always come down to communicating? In my opinion, it is because it's how the world goes around. The New Oxford Dictionary defines communication as the imparting or exchanging of information or news. Well, that includes everything right? Take a moment and make a mental list of all the unique ways you send and receive information. I'll help you get started: sight, sound, touch, and taste are your basic four senses that are being bombarded constantly with information. It is then up to you to interpret the news and information coming your way. When you use these four basic senses you also need to consider how you are communicating internally and externally. What I mean is how do you process and exchange the news and information coming your way?

News and information are just that, news and information. It is data void of all emotion when you boil it down and strip away what we attach to it or what others are attaching to it. For example, good news to one person is just news to another person. You must admit this and think about this before you can go farther. There are two types of communication: internal and external. One is not more important than the other because they affect each other with great significance. To me, internal and external importance lies with what comes first, the chicken or the egg discussion. For me, they both impact each other greatly, and if either is off and out of alignment it affects the other.

It was Saturday, January 11, 2020, and I was standing in Coral E of the Walt Disney World Half-Marathon ready to accomplish my goal of beating last year's time, which I wasn't proud of. I didn't care if it was by 30 seconds or two minutes. I just wanted to beat it. It was slightly warmer than I had hoped, but not too bad because it was supposed to stay overcast. I had been eating clean all week and had trained some (not as much as I should have), but not any less than I had the year before. I was about 10lbs lighter than in 2019 so I liked my odds. I did the math on the split times I needed, set the pace alerts on my watch to keep me ahead of my goal, and within the pace, I had been running during training. I got this. I downloaded the 3 of 7 podcast episode with Jesse Itzler where he was talking about running his 100-mile race and how he managed through the tough times by using techniques taught to him by the host, Chadd Wright and viewing your tongue as your rudder and not giving your pain (physical) a voice. I have everything ready... I say a prayer giving God the glory for being able to participate physically in an activity such as this, my coral is called, the fireworks go off, and then I cross the start line and hit start on my watch for a journey I was hoping would be over in less than 2 hours and 27 minutes.

If you have ever run any race, no matter the distance or your time, you will relate to everything I am about to describe. You should also be able to relate to the internal and external self-talk either way. Just put yourself into a past situation of difficulty that required endurance whether it was mental or physical, or in this case both. The first part of the race was going well. I was staying at my pace to beat my time by several minutes. I finished the podcast with great tips (I had listened to this episode before but I wanted to hear all the coaching again because I knew I would need it).

I'm around mile 6 and I notice my pace is slowing down but I still feel pretty good so I kick it back up a notch and I hear the negative thoughts creep in about being tired and beating myself up for not training enough, the typically fixed mindset self-critical internal communication that has held me back for most of my life, but I power through it. I say out loud, "I don't get tired" "I don't get tired." I keep saying this when my legs feel like concrete and they get better. Hey, this stuff really works! Then the dreaded mile nine. The weather is still good and I remember saying to myself, I can't use this as an excuse dang it, but I am running out of gas fast. I have now switched to saying out loud "I don't feel pain!" and "I don't get tired!" Mile ten gets a little better and then the next three miles just kick me in the teeth! I have never felt this exhaustion, and I have run this race for the past ten years. The "old" Jeff is being chattier than my 9-year-old daughter before bed. The internal voice is so loud so I talk again and I don't care who hears me. I'm proud mentally of what I'm pulling off and then I look at my watch and do the math, I won't beat my time or if I do, it'll be close. I pace myself on mile 12 to help me push hard through the end. I know I am not injured so the pain will be temporary but my body won't cooperate with me. The internal dialog is out of control at this point. It's like two heavyweight fighters going at it.

"Come on, just quit. You won't beat your time again!"

"Dude, don't listen to that garbage. You aren't hurt. Remember what Chadd and Jesse said."

"My legs are so heavy. You can just walk"

"Don't do it,"

"I don't want to stop but I have to" and it happened. I convinced myself to stop and walk some. I rationalized it in my head and I still don't think it was a mistake, but then the internal dialog started again,

"I knew you couldn't keep going!"

"Geez I can't win with you, so you know what, I will run again" and I did. I didn't care how slow I just knew I had to win this battle not against the clock but in my head. I have had battles like this before but not like this where I was really fighting back. I rounded the final corner where I could hear the crowd and the announcers at the finish line and I said out loud "I don't get tired" "I don't feel pain" "I am fast." I dug deep and gave it everything I had. I crossed that finish line and almost passed out! A nice lady greeting finishers came over and said with a scared look on her face "Are you ok?" "I think so. let me just hold on to this rail for a second." I gather myself and look at my watch...I didn't beat my time. I missed it by one minute. That's 4.5 seconds per mile. I learned so much in that race and I learned more by missing it by one minute than I would if I had beat my time by five minutes. The power of what you are saying to yourself and choose to say out loud will predict your future. 100% every time.

Let's take a few minutes and think about a few things:

- What type of communicator are you? To yourself and others?
- How do you like others to communicate with you?
- How much thought do you put into the words you say to yourself and others?
- What improvements can you make to be more effective in communicating?
- How can you think of others when you are communicating?

These questions will be the basis of the next two chapters and they are questions many of us just have put little thought into. These questions cover both internal and external communication. As you learned in my running example, what I said to myself out loud programmed what I thought inside.

Internal communication is what we are saying to ourselves over and over and it's how we interpret the outside world. For me, this is where change had to happen. If I wanted to change how I thought and to unleash my potential, I needed to reprogram my thoughts. I needed to shift from having a fixed mindset to a growth mindset. Many of the problems I was having with others started with how I was interpreting the information I was hearing from them. I will not accept all the blame, just like you shouldn't. Remember what I said earlier about news and information is just data stripped of emotion until we attach something to it? When I read a text or an email, I assign what I think they are saying versus just absorbing the data. Did I read it differently because I like or dislike the person? Do I read it differently because I'm upset or emotional? Therefore, our own internal communication is so important to pay attention to and correct.

If we can affect ourselves so much with what we say, how do you think we can impact other people when we don't know the internal dialogue they have after we say what we say and how we say it? It is so important to be mindful of how and what we say to others because once those words leave our mouth you can't take them back. Yes, you can apologize for them, but they can never be erased. I have heard from many authors and speakers I highly respect that if someone doesn't understand what we are saying it is not their fault; it is our own. When I first heard this, I didn't agree, but then I thought about it and realized how selfish and small-minded I was. Just because I say something doesn't mean everyone will understand it, and if I want to be an effective communicator I need to know my audience. I need to select the what and how I deliver the information I need to get across, and that takes effort and an intentional focus to do so. I need the humility that not everyone hears as I do. Therefore, the first two questions are so important. You need to understand you and then think about the other person next. The person you are communicating with needs to be the most important person to you. Your words and body language are telling your story while they are interpreting the information. So, are you focused on making sure it is clear and easy to understand? Are you being selfish and conceited in the words you say and how you say them? I know I sound harsh and I am intentionally doing so because I want a reaction from you. I want you to sit up a little and take notice. As a human, we all need to be aware of how and what we say to other people. Wars and peaceful revolutions are created and ended with external communication and how those words make us feel.

Hopefully, you will read and feel how important internal and external communication is to me and how being intentional on improving with both has shaped my new approach to life. Take a moment to think of how your favorite song, your favorite book, your favorite comedian, your favorite motivational clip on social media made you feel. Reflect on the words a gifted author uses to share an idea. How does an award-winning actor move you to tears? They do it by connecting the external to the internal intentionally. Some people have more natural ability than your average person but this skill can be learned and improved upon if you make it important. There are so many ways you can learn. You can listen to more speakers and podcasts or read more books and articles. You can even hire a coach or align with a mentor, but whatever you choose it should be intentional. You must want to improve because now you accept what has gotten you this far in life won't help you achieve more. True leaders and genius are always wanting to learn more and be more than what they are right at that moment. Is that you? Are you still wanting to unleash more of your potential? If you do, focus and be intentional about improving how you communicate to yourself and others. In my humble opinion, if you don't change how you communicate internally and externally you won't truly unlock your potential.

INTERNAL COMMUNICATION—WHAT DO YOU SAY TO YOURSELF?

"**I**'m not good enough,"

"People aren't interested in what I have to say."

"Don't write a book because everyone does and no one will read it."

These are things I told myself for about two years before a brilliant coach and mentor, Adam Davis, figuratively punched me in the nose with the words "you have to write a book, and here is what you need to do." I needed that kick in the butt to get out of my head. Why was I worried about that nonsense? Why was I answering questions for others? Fear that's why. How many internal thoughts we have come from fear or based on past experiences? All of them. It is what we do as humans. Our internal dialogue comes from the epigenetics of past generations that have programmed us to think and act a certain way, but that thought pattern isn't a life sentence. We can change our thinking if we choose to. I know I had a victim mentality most of my life because it is a superb way to avoid anything that is difficult.

To change internal thoughts, it takes a lot of focus and intentional work because this internal communication results from years and years of situations we have endured and survived through. Think about it for a minute, I have heard from a young age to clean my plate. "Don't waste food!" So, what do I do when my kids don't eat their pizza crust or leave a couple of chicken nuggets on the plate? I eat them because I feel bad "wasting" food. I hear the voice telling me to eat it even after I have eaten my fair share of food. I battle with myself to just leave it but I do it anyway. Why do we do that? How can we stop eating the pizza crust off our kid's plates?

Dr. Thurman Fleet explored how the mind works and the impact of how the conscious mind impacts the subconscious and thus manifests in the body which leads to action and results. This is often referred to as the 'Stick Man.'

The conscious mind is the thinking mind. It

represents our free will and our IQ. This is where intentional self-talk must happen if you are looking to reprogram an action or behavior. This is you taking control of your thoughts internally and externally. To unleash our potential, we have to use our free will/conscious mind to go to work for us. Our subconscious is our emotional mind that runs our lives. This can be dangerous if left unattended. The subconscious is where your self-image lives, your experiences, good or bad, and your habits. The subconscious doesn't know if it's the right thing to do, it just knows to do it. Each thought our conscious mind accepts automatically is accepted by our subconscious. It has no choice. Thoughts create feelings, feelings create actions, and this leads to our attitude. Therefore, habits eat willpower for lunch. We can't trust our subconscious to choose what's right for us because it only knows what we have been telling it.

I am using Dr. Fleet's "Stick Man" as an example of the power of the internal and external communication we have with ourselves and since this is a book focused on helping to unleash your potential, you have to understand what it will take on your part to change your own internal and external thinking. You possess the power to accept or reject a thought/situation and once you accept this, you will stop blaming others. I know I did and you know what, I took my power back from all the mistakes I made, big and small, and I gained more power from the good decisions I made. Bottom line... I'm more powerful for understanding I'm in control! You control your awareness which reveals your potential.

Dr. Fleet shares that your subconscious controls your body which controls your results, and I couldn't agree more. I think back to when I lost a lot of weight. I was focused on what I should and shouldn't eat and this controlled what I put in my body, which that led to the result of losing weight. I wasn't aware of Dr. Fleet's stick man theory back then but it was 100% how I accomplished my goal. On the opposite end, it is also why I never lost weight before. I had allowed myself and others to program my thoughts to accept the fact "I was born this way," so I just ate what I wanted because I didn't think it would matter. So do you believe in the importance of what you say to yourself and how it affects your results?

The importance of the "inner" thinking is also revealed and discussed at length in a splendid book by W. Timothy Gallwey, *The Inner Game of Tennis*. In it, Gallwey states, "The basics of the inner game are very, simple, ancient, and there are no magical shortcuts to establishing harmony between mind and body. Individuals must do the work within themselves. Good coaching can help; I hope this book can help, but learning to get out of one's own way, the goal of the inner game, must come from the experience of each player who has the courage and determination to attempt it." (pg. xii forward) The last part of that quote is the most important part. "The courage and determination to attempt it." I know for me this was and still is the most difficult because I find I make excuses for myself and why I chose to not do something. I am becoming more accountable to myself, which is shaping who I am on the outside and how I externally communicate. Look, this will be hard and you will fail many times while you are changing how you communicate with yourself internally, but if you really want to unleash your potential and stop being "ordinary" this is a requirement.

The way I started changing the internal dialog was by making minor changes, agreeing this transformation will take time and energy, and using the way I externally communicated with myself. Go grab those post-it notes you were using for the strengths and weakness exercise. Got them? Good! The first step is to think about how you communicate with yourself internally. What does the daily dialogue in your head sound like? Are you annoyed that you can't keep a promise to yourself? Do you want to stop sneaking those extra cookies in between meals but can't? Do you want to go to the gym but you keep talking yourself out of going? Do you accept that it is just the way God made you? This is just how my family is? (mark the page and take a few minutes to think about this. What do you say to yourself?) Think about all the things you want to do but won't because you accept excuses you or others have made for you. See how I didn't say can't? Can't and won't are different and there are so many times we say can't when we mean won't. This is where you should admit how you speak to yourself and change. Be honest with yourself inside and out.

We are focusing on changing your internal communication, and you change this through how you communicate with yourself externally. This is where this chapter crosses over into the next one on external communication because you can't change the inside without the help of the outside. Dr. Fleet shared that it is your conscious thought that programs your subconscious, and the subconscious is where your habits live. You must commit to intentionally working on this and paying close attention to it because you are worth it!

On your first post-it note write, "I am worth it!" and stick it somewhere you will see multiple times per day. I used the mirror in my bathroom so I would see it first thing in the morning and the last thing before I went to bed.

I read *Can't Hurt Me* by David Goggins and he speaks about his use of the accountability mirror and how it changed his life. I followed the steps he shared, and it dramatically affected me. I still use these techniques two years later. He suggests looking at yourself in the eye and being honest with yourself, then changing the narrative you created for yourself. I won't go into all the details, but read the book if you haven't because there are some great tips in there for getting more out of your life.

Back to the post-it and the mirror. Look at that note "I am worth it" and say it out loud; trust me, over the course of a few days you will stand taller, smile bigger, and people will take notice. We aren't usually very nice to ourselves and it's about time you are. You are worth it. The world needs the best version of you and we can't have you holding yourself back. Whether you believe you are worth it yet, keep saying it out loud. I'm serious. Forget about what you think someone else will think when you say it. Be bold and say "I am worth it." If you start there for the first week you will be excited about what comes next. I don't have a magic formula for this, just things I have done that have changed me and I know they will help you. Some other notes I still have on my mirror are "Make a difference in someone's life today," "Add value," "God won't reject me," "Be decisive," "Be active daily," and "Floss daily." Yes, floss daily has been one I am very proud of because it is simple but powerful because it is a habit I know I created and never had before. I literally have flossed every day for the past 8 months and hadn't done that ever in my life. I may have flossed 8 times in two years. This is how I know focusing on minor changes will make a big impact that far reaches just wanting to keep my teeth!

You may need to write a note holding you accountable for reading and saying your notes out loud. When I first started with the notes, I had them all around my mirror. I mean there were a ton of them everywhere, but I was a mess and needed them. I had no focus. I was full of excuses for why I couldn't do things or just avoided them altogether. I was so weak-minded I didn't even approach the subject of improving something, just shame. Another one that stood out was eating French fries. I LOVE French fries so much! I would justify eating them often, too. Too often really. I wrote on a post-it note, "Don't eat French fries" and I didn't. I would allow myself a Saturday here and there but I was ok with that because I was holding myself accountable for making a change with my internal justification dialogue that was leading to unhealthy decisions. Find ways to make small wins and allow them to compound into larger ones. Again, this worked for me and may not for you, but it's worth a shot if you aren't satisfied with where you are at right now.

As I accomplished changing and creating a new habit I took them down, and sometimes I had to write them down again and put them back up because I backslid a bit. It's ok because I'm in this for the long run. Another fun tip is taking advantage of the alarms of reminders function in your phone. I have set multiple alarms daily in my phone and changed the label so when it goes off I know what I need to do and this has even affected my family. I want to be more present and appreciative of my family so I set a daily alarm for 7 pm labeled "hug your family", so every night at 7 pm no matter where we are at we stop what we are doing and if we are together we hug each other and at the least, I think about hugging them which makes me appreciate them.

Get creative in changing the way you conduct your internal communication to make the biggest impact on your improvement. The post-it notes or alarms on your phone might not be your thing and that's fine, but it doesn't give you an excuse to not think of what will work for you. If you are saying post-it notes or alarms won't work for you, take a moment and think about why you say that. Are you just creating an excuse because it sounds hard or tedious? Are you scared of the work it will take to make some necessary changes? Are you scared if you fail at first trying to make these changes? These things are valid concerns but not excuses to not start trying some of these tactics to improve your life.

I know for a fact the words you say to yourself out loud directly affect your internal communication, so whatever you have to do to change that, do that. A great friend and mentor Chadd Wright says, "Your tongue is your rudder" and he is spot on. Be careful where you allow your rudder to steer your ship. I'll go back to the example of my run when I was so tired. If I would have said out loud, "I'm tired," I would have walked the rest of the way and not only not beat my time from the previous year, but would have lost the battle in my head.

EXTERNAL COMMUNICATION-WHAT DO YOU SAY TO OTHERS?

"Go clean your room and it better be spotless!"

I have two children. My daughter is nine and my son is twelve and whenever my wife and I are the most frustrated, is when the kids aren't following directions. But this frustrates the kids, too. Does this sound similar? Have you thought about who's to blame? Is it the kid's fault for not following the directions we provided, or is it our fault for not providing easy to follow directions? Marinate on that one. For me, I make assumptions that simple directions I can follow are directions that a 12 or 9-year-old can follow. Well, they don't have the experience and background information to make decisions on loose instruction, they need to have specific directions. What does

"Go clean your room and it better be spotless" mean to you? I know it is different for me than it is for my wife, and it is different for you I bet too. Think about it? I know this is a simple exercise and I want to get you thinking of how you will interpret a vague set of instructions like I gave you and we give to others all the time.

When was the last time you thought about the words you say to others? Are you guilty of not thinking about the audience and what it will take for you to communicate with them in an effective manner? Are you frustrated when someone doesn't deliver the results you want? If you are anything like me, I didn't think about the words I was saying and how I said them until about ten years ago. I had some public speaking courses in college that made me more aware when I was speaking in a formal environment, but not much when I was just speaking one on one. I would say how you are going to speak to another person is far more important than when you are on stage, because how often are you asked to speak on stage? What you say, how you say it, and your body language when you are communicating to someone one on one will have a large ripple effect on the relationship with that person and their relationships with others.

There is a wonderful book by Marshall Goldsmith

and Mark Reiter entitled, *What Got You Here Won't Get You There: How Successful People Become Even More Successful.* This book bases most of its teachings on the importance of external communication and interpersonal behaviors. We are going to focus on external communication. We must pay attention to how our words impact other people because as I stated in the previous chapter, people will interpret the words for themselves without understanding your intentions, so you need to be clear.

These are just several from a list of 20 that jump out to me. I've implemented them in my life, and, by doing so, I have seen and continue to see positive effects (Goldsmith, p40).

- Winning at all costs: the need to win in everything even when it doesn't matter. This one came up for me out of just trying to connect to someone. They would share a story about a vacation or a situation they had, and I had to "one" up their story or at least make a comment on how I did the same thing. I thought about it and I bet most people do this and not out of trying to one-up the other person, but it still comes across that way because you are shifting the focus away from them and on to you. Just be aware and allow the other person to shine and you can make comments such as, "I loved going to New York," versus telling your entire story that shifts focus away from them.

Another great example of winning at all costs many people don't think about is when someone sends you a text or an email with an article, facts, jokes, or a funny meme you have already seen and your quick response is "I just saw that" or "I saw that last week" this blows up the confidence and excitement the other person has for trying to provide value to you. A simple thank you is enough. If you respond with "already saw that" too many times, people will stop sending you things. Think about how your external communication will affect someone else.

- Adding too much value: the overwhelming desire to add our two cents to every discussion. This is one that comes up all the time and I don't think most people are doing it to intentionally one-up the other person: however, it comes across that way. Most people have a hard time accepting that someone else has an idea first or even suggests an idea they already have so they make the comment, "I already tried that" "I've known that already." By adding too much value to lift your self-worth and self-image, you are smashing someone else's along the way and this will stifle creativity and people making suggestions. We need other people's ideas because we don't have all the answers.

- Making destructive comments: The needless sarcasm and cutting remarks that we think make us sound sharp and witty. This one is straight forward, but challenging for many people to overcome. I used to be guilty of this one because I wanted to be witty and funny, to connect with others and to have my self-image to feel better by subconsciously putting others down. I felt like I was gaining traction with the group when I was pushing people further away. One way to know if you are doing this is if you are saying "I was just kidding" or "Boy, everyone is so sensitive." Stop trying to make yourself look bigger by putting others down.

- Starting with "No", "But" or "However":

The overuse of these negative qualifiers which secretly say to everyone, "I'm right and you're wrong." This is a big one, I know, I was guilty of before I read this book back in 2012. Take some time and listen to other people and how they use it."I like how you cooked the steak, but I would have liked it to have a little more salt." That is just a very general example. The first part means nothing but the person who was saying it was trying to be "nice," but, they just communicated they didn't like the steak how it was served. There are so many opportunities you can use "and" to accomplish the same thing and add more value to the other person. I was in sales leadership and training for many years and I can't count how many times I was guilty of using "but" without thinking about it. "You did great during that call, but next time you should do this." Do you think the person was open to the suggestions since I just told them their way wasn't any good and they needed to try it my way? The reaction I normally received was defensive and them defending why they did it the way they did. After being made aware of my improper use of the word "but," I pivoted and gained more impact and positive response to the coaching. My new phrase sounded more like this, "You did great during that call and next time you could be more direct..." See how it sounds and feels different. The person did a great job so allow them to know it and feel it. Our conversation was great because it then formed into a brainstorming session on other ideas they came up with on how they could add to their discussion. I want you, the reader, to think about how you are using these negative qualifiers and don't even realize it. These simple words will shape how someone receives the words you are speaking or sending in a text or email.

- Clinging to the past: the need to deflect blame away from ourselves and onto events and people from our past: a subset of blaming everyone else. Now, this one is so deep I will leave it to an entire book of its own one day. Our past is our past and we need to learn from it and accept it as a necessary event to teach us a valuable lesson. Marcus Aurelius wrote in *Meditations* 5.8, "Because the whole is damaged if you cut away anything— anything at all—from its continuity and its coherence. Not only its parts, but its purposes. And that's what you're doing when you complain: hacking and destroying."

You just read some critical aspects about how the words we use to communicate can be interpreted by others negatively, and now I want to shift your thoughts to lifting others up. Putting more thought into how you make people feel will not only help you connect with others better, but it will also change you as a person and communicator. Positive and uplifting words and actions are rarely misinterpreted incorrectly. They may be suspicious if it's not how you normally treat others, but they will be pleasantly surprised.

Remember in the previous chapter we reviewed Doctor Thurman's "Stickman" and how the words we speak out loud change our subconscious that leads to different actions and results? It does, and not just in how you are combating the internal voice we deal with, but how we speak to others. The more we speak positivity and encouragement to others, it will change us. Now, this is easier said than done. This takes focus and being intentional in the words we say. How do you make others feel?

How do your body language and facial expression make them feel? Do you try to smile when you see someone on the street? These are all subtle ways you are impacting others either in a positive or negative way.

For me, I added a post-it note to my mirror and list on my daily goal sheet "to make others feel good." This is an intentional focus of mine for the past year and I know I have changed. My thoughts are focused more on others and lifting them up, which in turn I have become more positive within myself. Now I have always been a positive and supportive person, but still tended to gossip and judge other people negatively. Gossip and judging others negatively in no way is encouraging to someone else, and it also tells the person I am gossiping to that I probably talk about them, too. I have started a conversation in my head to ask, "is this uplifting the person I'm about to speak about, or am I about to say something that puts me in a better light than them?" The more I shift away from not speaking this way, I have noticed, the fewer people are bringing gossip to me. I'm not naïve to the fact they are probably just going to someone else, but maybe, just maybe, this is helping shape their outlook towards others as well.

This is where I ask you to keep an open mind because all of this is external communication could be holding you back from unleashing your potential and standing out from the rest. Along with the words you are using to communicate, your body language is communicating as well. There are plenty of books and experts out there, way more educated on this than I am, so I will keep my thoughts brief and present ideas for you to consider and ponder on.

I have deeper set eyes and a natural frown so many have told me I look unapproachable. Geez, that hurts, but it's how others are interpreting my body language and how they see me. It's part of my external communication. This was vital feedback for me because if you know me, I am the last person you should be intimated by. I started to do some reading on body language tips and one was to practice opening your eyes wider to make yourself look less angry. It's a weird feeling because I feel like I am opening them so wide people will think I look bug-eyed, but when I try it and look in the mirror, I look just fine and it works. When I focus on opening my eyes wider, it naturally lifts my entire face, which is helping my smile. I then focus on smiling more, and people notice which makes me feel better. These are two very simple adjustments that can be made, that can have large impacts on others and yourself.

John Maxwell said it best when he said, "A person

that can get their ideas across to others will have success." Mr. Maxwell also suggests that if someone isn't understanding what you are trying to communicate, it isn't their problem, it is yours. This was a difficult concept for me to agree with, but the more I thought about it the more I must agree. Think about what you just read in this chapter. It's all about you! There is no passing the buck to the other person. Now I want you to think back to the beginning of this chapter, to the instructions I gave my kids, "Go clean your room, and it better be spotless!"

How could you provide more clear instruction to someone that would set them up for success? Think it through. Take a deep breath. This is on you and not them. I'll go first.

"Kids, I need both of you to clean up your rooms, and here is what I need you to do.

1. Make your bed and I will show you what is acceptable.
2. Pick up all your clothes and put the dirty ones in the laundry basket and the clean ones folded in the drawers or hung up in the closet.
3. Pick up your toys and put them back where they belong, and if you don't then

you cannot play the iPad the rest of the week."

This leaves no room for interpretations in my opinion. I know my 12-year-old will challenge me and that's fine. I was clear and calm and he has the proper explanation of what I am asking him to do and the consequence if he doesn't follow those instructions. Let me tell you that life is way better now because I am learning that I am responsible for how I communicate. I am also teaching both my children the same thing when they are communicating with others.

We must embrace that we are all communicators no matter our age or our position in life. As I stated in the previous chapter, it starts with how we are communicating with ourselves. Focus there first and find how you can change you for the better and once you start that process, you can layer in how your communication with others will impact you and them.

If the words in this book aren't connecting with you, it's not your fault. It's mine!

DON'T DEPEND ON ANYONE ELSE TO DEVELOP YOU!

I share plenty of stories about my children and in this chapter, it won't be any different. I share these stories because everyone reading this book either has children now, had children previously, or was a child. We have all been there!

It's Saturday morning at 7:30 AM, and my kids are bumping around the house and pretty much sitting on their bottoms in front of the TV or on their tablet watching some mind-numbing video on the internet. Sound familiar? From the couch I hear, "Daddy, I'm hungry. Will you make me some breakfast?" Previously, I would without hesitation make them breakfast because of their age (I still make breakfast for them because I enjoy it, but that's not the point). Now they are 9 and 12 and it's important for them to start learning how to make breakfast for themselves, so I respond with one of two typical parent responses. "Are your legs broken?" or "If you are hungry, you need to get up and make it yourself!"

So why as parents are we encouraging our children to make their own breakfast or get their own snacks? We are doing it to teach them self-reliance because we won't always be there to do everything for them. If we don't allow them to learn at a young age, they will grow dependent on others or the system to provide for them. There comes a time when we must force our children to grow up and make their own breakfast. This also pertains to self-development. How many of us are going through our personal lives and professional career expecting someone else to "make our breakfast" for us?   In my experience, the vast majority. I have led and trained many teams made up of all personality types, and so many people are content with where they are or expect to be handed everything; however, they are upset if they don't achieve the career progression they expect. That sounds kind of odd as you read this, right? They don't want to put forth any self-discipline or self-initiative to take advantage of training offered, but are disappointed when they are told they don't have the skills the advanced position requires. One of the skills every leader looks for is self-discipline and self-initiative. I want someone who puts in the extra effort when no one is looking. Take two of the greatest athletes of my generation, Mia Hamm and Kobe Bryant (sorry for always using sports references). Both athletes are world-class and known for the training and effort they put in when no one else was looking. They were never content. Yes, they had unbelievable natural talent, but they also had a natural drive and growth mindset unmatched by many.

"The vision of a champion is bent over, drenched in sweat, at the point of exhaustion when nobody else is looking," Mia Hamm.

You cannot delegate your own self-development. You cannot wait for someone else to give you what you need because they don't know what you need. You can't sit back and wait for someone to schedule training for you if you want to unleash your true potential. You must be intentional with what you want to work on and what you want to achieve. If I want to learn how to play the piano, what will it take? I won't accidentally be able to play anything, even chopsticks. I need to sit down and learn it. I don't even need someone in person to teach me. I do need a piano or keyboard though. I must make up my mind, sit down, look up how to play the chopsticks on the internet, and practice. It won't take that long because chopsticks aren't that difficult.

If you remember in chapter five, I spoke about the importance of internal and external self-talk and how you can program yourself to accomplish things you never wanted to or thought you were able to. Well, that chapter is strategically placed before this one because self-development personally and professionally requires you to be intentional on how you talk to yourself. Take me for instance, I used to whine and complain about physical training or even learning. I hated practicing and learning. I didn't see the need in it, but when it came game time I beat myself up because I didn't perform and obtain the results I wanted. Just like the half marathon I mentioned, but over time I have started to understand "I get what I pay for." I didn't pay the price to obtain the results, and it's arrogant of me to think otherwise.

Decide today if you are willing to put in the work to commit to your own self-development. This isn't a half in, half out commitment. You should start telling yourself you want to put in the hard work and the hard work is where the glory is. The glory is not in the desired result! This book won't make you unleash your potential. No book will. You are the only person who can intentionally put in the work to unleash the potential you know you have.

You can start by looking back through your personal and professional life and make a timeline of development. Intentionally take out a piece of paper and draw a line. I don't care if it is vertical or horizontal but draw a line from one end to the other and start making tick marks on the line and add in the times you put in the work to get better, what you did during those times and the results. If you are anything like me, I can't remember everything the first time through so take your time and look it over several times. All the exercises rely on you being honest and not judging yourself. The past is the past. You picked up this book because you want to make a change, and that is awesome!

When I do my timeline, I'm amazed at the work I put in and it also brings up the times when I had a terrible fixed mindset. I'm convinced some of us are born with a growth mindset and others like me a fixed mindset. Now, I don't think I came out of the womb with a fixed mindset but the environment we are raised in and exposed to will create this, for we have a tendency to lean one way or the other. This chapter isn't about our mindset so I don't want to chase that rabbit, but it is important to realize those times YOU held yourself back. Yes, you held yourself back, and I could name tons of people throughout history who had the cards stacked against them, yet they unleashed their potential and accomplished remarkable things. Yours and my biggest issue was and is making excuses. See how all this stuff ties together?

I'll provide you an example of what I am talking about. My career was at a standstill. I had been a sales rep for the better part of seven years. I had a couple of shots of getting the development and career advancement I had wanted, only to have my manager change each time which I thought caused me to start over. Oh, poor me! I complained to anyone who would listen. "I never catch a break." "This company or manager won't give me the development I need to advance my career." There are not enough pages in this chapter to list all the excuses I made, at least the ones I remember. Because of my life experiences, I did have a lot of natural leadership skills, but had not matured the skills I needed most- self-discipline and humility. In fact, I expected to have "my breakfast made for me," and when someone didn't make it for me, that is when the victim mentality kicked in.

I hit obstacles along the way, but I must have been ok with them because I did very little to get around them. I used them as an excuse to avoid the real hard work of self-development. I had every opportunity to seek help from outside mentors, books, CDs, training seminars (this was the early

2000s and podcasts and YouTube didn't exist yet), but didn't. During this time, I did not take ownership in my own personal development. I was delegating it out to her and complaining about it. I felt people in a supervisory role have a responsibility to identify blind spots for people they are responsible for and help them gain the development they require. That's why we call them blind spots, because the individual doesn't see them, but we cannot rely on developing our own. We should look for other resources if we see we aren't getting what we need.

Throughout time, there have always been resources available for those who wanted to be more. Resources were limited, but they were there for people who wanted to find them. My father's generation had libraries filled with books, lectures live and on record (I mean Zig Ziglar started speaking in 1963), mentors, teachers, coaches, friends, and parents. This generation had the ability to learn, but they had to really go get it. They seriously had to "make their own breakfast" because it was a different time. Very little was given to anyone. If you wanted something, you had to do it all on your own.

Take my generation, the Gen Xers. We saw the modernization of learning start with the advent of the cassette tape and digital media on CDs that could easily travel with you on your vibrant yellow portable cassette/CD player with headphones. Self-development started to become simpler and more recognized. I started seeing ads on television for self-development gurus offering sets of their seminars on VHS tapes. Now you wouldn't have to travel to a specific destination to gain the development you needed. You could sit in front of your television and watch it as many times as you wanted. One drawback was the expense (excuse that I always used) of these VHS sets. Then in the mid-90s, the internet became more accessible and started opening doors for the masses because the information was easier and more cost-effective to deliver, which exposed more people.

Never has there been a better time to have free resources at our fingertips. There is so much content between the social media apps, podcasts, more books on every topic you can imagine, self-development apps, YouTube®, online masterminds, seminars, on-line tribes, virtual coaches, and I could go on and on and on. We have zero excuses to make about personal development, but we still make them. We make them because of our self-talk and programming.

"I don't have enough time."

"When I have the time, I will sit down and do that."

"Ugh, I need to read that book, listen to that podcast, watch that video."

"I should reach out to that professional development coach I heard about."

"I need to find a mentor."

These are all things I have said at one time or the other. All of these are excuses, and bad ones at that. I had programmed myself to not make the time for what is most important, my self-development. I cannot and will not blame anyone else for my lack of development and neither should you. There are so many books, podcasts, videos, and mentors where you could learn about time management. We all have 24 hours in our day and 7 days in our week and 365 days in our year (yes, I know leap year has 366. Go with me on this one, I'm on a roll) and how we use it is up to us.

I thought about breaking down the day by how many hours you do each activity, but I don't think that's fair because everyone's day-to-day is unique and I don't want you tuning out on me just yet. Just take an inventory of your day for a week and see where you can find just two hours a week to apply towards self-development. With the right time management techniques, I know you can find even more time. With two hours per week of intentional self-development where you apply what you see, read, or hear, you will see incremental improvements to unleashing your potential.

Don't limit yourself to just watching, listening, and reading because there is no substitute to an excellent coach/mentor. These are people you find that can and will help you learn skills and avoid obstacles they encountered along their path. Sometimes, you will find someone who will help you for free and that is great, but don't avoid investing in yourself. You are your best investment, and what I have found out about myself is that I don't pay attention to something as much as I should unless I pay for it. How do you think I learned how to write a book, for Pete's sake? I hired a coach, Adam Davis. What is great is that I initially hired him to help me learn about digital marketing because I knew nothing about it. I didn't have the patience to sit and look up all the information on the internet and then filter through what would work and what wouldn't. Adam was very skilled in this area and came highly recommended by some very influential people. I had also heard Adam on several podcasts I listen to and purchased one of his devotional books,

Bulletproof Marriage. After the first call he had already made suggestions which would improve my website, and on our second call, he stopped the discussion and said "Brother, you need to write a book!" Adam pivoted our coaching calls from digital marketing to steps to getting started writing a book. I may have written a book at some point (doubtful), but it wouldn't have been as enjoyable without Adam's experience and motivation. I needed Adam to help me and you should find your own "Adam" to help coach you through your blind spots or weaknesses. I bet you pay a gym for group classes or have a stationary bike at home with a TV connected to a trainer to help you improve your fitness, so why not hire someone to help you personally or professionally?

I heard a great saying a couple of years ago. The more you learn, the more you will love learning. It is a never-ending cycle that will have you accomplishing more than you ever thought you were capable of.

WHO DO YOU SURROUND YOURSELF WITH?

"You are the average of the five people you spend the most time with."

This is a quote by the great Jim Rohn and I agree with it 100%. It is also a lesson that has been around since the beginning of time. There are so many lessons in the Bible, from the Stoics, and many more people from history emphatic about this point. This doesn't just include your family, close friends, or tribe you experienced life with, but also the teachers, coaches, mentors, and confidants. We need these people to support, but also to challenge, push, motivate, and learn from. If you find that you are the smartest person in your group, in my mind there are two problems. First, find a new group of people who will push you to be more than you are, or second, and most likely, you are far too arrogant because you can learn from anyone when you will listen and learn. It all depends on the subject you are trying to learn.

I'll provide an example of what I mean by this. As you can tell by now, I am a tremendous fan of my family, and I have listened and learned from my kids. Just as a reminder, at the time I am writing this my son is 12 and my daughter is nine. About eight months ago, my son and I were having a conversation about his upcoming fall Little League baseball season and the importance of practicing with the team and on his own. I was on a roll explaining this and that when he hit me with a right cross of wisdom. "Dad, one of the hardest things to do, other than doing, is practicing." Boom! I was so taken aback by the power of that statement I grabbed my phone and jotted it down in the notes app. Think about that statement for a second. It means so much to the theme of this book, but also how my 11-year-old son just dropped wisdom on me. This young man can also be a mentor if I listen and not let the father/son dynamic get in the way.

I haven't always been smart in who I surrounded myself with, but many people have done this also. We have all fallen victim to linking up with someone who may have been fun to hang out with but just wasn't someone who made us a better person as it pertained to our faith, our family, or our physical or mental health. People like this bring our average down and being candid, how many times have I been that person for someone else? I can think of several times where I was in a negative headspace and needed company, so I used my influence to pull them down with me. It is so easy to either follow someone or lead someone down a path of being negative and unproductive. Let us reflect on this for a moment. Are you or have you been the one who picks up the phone or as soon as you see someone at the store talks about someone else and what happened to them, or just something negative about someone else? I have and I chose to intentionally focus on stopping that because it is unproductive for me, the person I am speaking with, and the person I am speaking about. Remember what Deuce said? "One of the hardest things to do, other than doing, is practicing," and when I wanted to change how I affected other people's average I had to practice, and boy is it hard.

I am discussing all of this because this chapter is about who you are surrounding yourself with, and I will touch on the importance of friends or a tribe, a mentor, a coach, and a confidant. Each one of these can and most likely will overlap, and they are so important to you unleashing your full potential.

I want to now describe how everyone needs each one of these to unleash their potential.

YOUR TRIBE

One definition from the Oxford Dictionary defines tribe as a distinctive or close-knit group. A tribe of like-minded individuals is so important to individual growth because a well-crafted tribe will fill your weakness gaps and assist you in unleashing your potential.

I also believe you can call a tribe a team if you want, because a well-crafted team operates the same way. This would be your close-knit group. For me, I am a big tribe or team guy. If you remember back to the personality section, I am a high S, which is all about team. I thrive in a team because I like to see others succeed. Not everyone is as tribe or team-oriented as I am, and I understand that, but being surrounded by a tribe and knowing there are like-minded people out there to help and support me is valuable. Even the toughest of the tough have tribes of like-minded people around them. I am learning how to build a tribe around me, and the first step for me was to put my ego in my back pocket.

For the majority of my life, I wanted a tribe to prop me up and be more of a cheer squad, and this is great; however, if I am surrounded by people just telling me how great I am or always clapping for everything I do, I won't grow. I'll still have my blind spots and a good tribe helps identify those for you and encourages growth. One point I want to get across is to assemble a tribe built to challenge you to become better and not to hide your weaknesses. It has happened to all of us; we align ourselves with people who prey on our weaknesses and take advantage of them. I grew up with low self-esteem and self-image. I just wanted to be accepted and would change who I was to just fit in. That's an equation for disaster, because if you are not true to yourself how can you ever unleash your true potential? My tribe is now one built of people I trust and admire who will shoot me straight, or at least just challenge my idea, sincerely because they want to see me succeed. They want the tribe to succeed.

My second tribe is distinctive. I like this one because this is my "secret tribe" and they aren't even aware of each other. Now, I don't do this intentionally, but it has worked out this way. These are people I highly respect but don't think they will fit into my close-knit group I described above. There may be differences socially or spiritually;

they wouldn't connect with the others or vice versa, and that's ok. They probably don't have me in their close-knit tribe either. These are also people I don't speak with on a regular basis, but consider them experts in an area that if I need to run something by them they are there and will provide a fresh perspective to the situation.

While you are assembling your tribe, whether it is distinctive or close-knit, members will probably come and go and that is fine. One may start out in the close-knit group and for whatever reason move into the distinct tribe I mentioned, or it could happen the other way around. Just constantly learn from them and why they didn't blend as well as others did. Don't link up with people who are just like you. Look for people who have traits you wish you had and be aware of how they will help you grow. This is one of the many reasons knowing your strengths and weaknesses is so important. Where do you fit on the team? Where can you help others and where do you need the most help? See what I mean about putting your ego in your back pocket? A tribe is intended to provide strength in numbers. In a successful tribe, there is no one person more important than the other.

MENTOR

The Oxford Dictionary defines a mentor as an experienced and trusted advisor. I love the description of a trusted advisor because how many of those do we have? I know for me I had some but my poor self-image prevented me from taking more advantage of them. I know I keep going back to my self-image and self-esteem and I am not beating myself, but trying to challenge you to think about yourself and why you may not be taking advantage or holding yourself back. I bet it's internal and not external. Mentors are all around us and don't even necessarily know they are mentoring us. I consume a large volume of content from authors, podcasters, and interviews and each of these people are mentoring me because they are sharing their story and how they managed through certain situations they encountered. This is incredibly valuable, and it means there are zero excuses for not having a mentor today.

I have heard from many different people of influence who describe a mentoring relationship as one where both people are involved and there is mutual benefit. I have two great friends- you know one of those friends that you want in your fox hole with you because they're awesome and would jump in front of a bullet for you- and their names are Butch and Raffaele. Raff, as most would know him as, and Butch are two of my mentors because of the relationship we have. Raff and I connect on a spiritual level even though we believe in different things. We just get each other, and what makes this friendship and valuable mentoring relationship is we both challenge and learn from one another. Butch and I met as we both entered pharmaceuticals more than 20 years ago at the same time, and that is when the bromance started. This dude has been with me through everything over the past 20 plus years and I couldn't have done it without him. These relationships aren't instructional by nature, where one person is the teacher and the other the student (I'll describe that in the coach/instructor section) because we both offer a lot to one another. These relationships are more than normal friendships as well. These two men have strength in areas I am not that strong in and vice versa. We help each other. We help each other grow and unleash our potential and it all just happened. I never picked up the phone and asked them to be my mentor, and they never did that to me either. I describe these relationships to shed light on the mentors you already have and may not have realized it.

I think it is critical for a proper mentoring relationship to evolve organically because in my opinion if you formalize with the words "Would you be open to being my mentor," you change the dynamics into teacher/student. If you respect someone's opinion and experience just pick up the phone. Call them and invite them to have coffee and start asking them questions. Learn from them and I bet they will start learning from you, because I guarantee you know more about something than they do. Let the relationship bloom into you both being trusted advisors to one another.

COACH/INSTRUCTOR

The Oxford Dictionary defines a coach as an instructor or trainer, and this is where people start to confuse a coach and a mentor. You can have a mentor who at times is a coach, and then you can also have a coach who becomes a mentor; but when you have a coach their priority is to help you grow and, just like having a tribe and a mentor, everyone should have a coach.

There are people we need to learn from and who need to teach us things. Flashback to the previous chapter when I described my coach/instructor Adam Davis. I would not be writing this book without his instruction. An instructor provides the tools necessary to do a job or a task in a more efficient and effective way. My dad always taught me the job is always easier when you have the right tools. Let me describe this with cutting down a tree. You can cut down a tree with a chainsaw or a hand saw. A chainsaw makes the job exponentially faster than with a hand saw, but you can cut the tree down with either. Taking it a step further, I can figure out how to cut a tree down with said chainsaw, but can I do it safely and efficiently on my own? I can get lucky and get the tree down but how much better would it be if I had a skilled woodsman instruct me on the proper way to have a tree cut and fall with precision? Many of us have the right tools to get the job done and it does not seem like a monumental task like cutting down a tree with a handsaw, but do we have the proper instruction to get the job done with efficiency and the least amount of damage. This is another relationship that required me to put my ego in my back pocket. I had to admit I didn't know how to do something and needed help. Now some people choose to figure out things on their own and that is awesome! I, however, learn better from visual and verbal instruction if I want to retain and add the skill to my tool kit. I am also a tad impatient to try to figure it out on my own. I embrace that about myself, and that way I try not to waste time or give me an excuse.

I also believe a true coach is different from an

instructor. A proper coach is focused solely on the success of the other person and to help the participant learn how to come up with a solution on their own. The power is in the relationship and not either person. These are meaningful conversations driven by questions the coach asks the participant. There is a genuine curiosity about who you are and who you want to be. This is so much different than that of an instructor. Coaches typically don't offer advice unless specifically given permission to because they aren't looking to be an instructor. A good coach also holds the participant to specific goals and timelines because many times they are more committed to the success of the participant than they are in themselves. I also will say a good coach creates a safe and non-judgmental environment. I know as I am describing this you are thinking this sounds a lot like a mental health therapist, and it's close, but don't be confused because most coaches are not and should not offer any mental health advice because they are not trained to do so. A coach should prepare you on how to handle things moving forward and not just dealing with your past. They are bringing awareness to situations and opportunities and assist you in developing a well thought out approach to those situations and opportunities.

CONFIDANT

The Oxford Dictionary defines a confidant as a person with whom one shares a secret or private matter, trusting them not to repeat it to others. This is by far the most powerful and life changing relationship that is shared through time. I can't stress this enough that you need to find someone who is judgement free and who you can share anything and everything with, and if you are like me I struggled with this big time. In my head, I condemned myself to being judged by everyone before I even shared anything. I had made the agreement inside myself that if I shared my secret fears and struggles I would be judged, looked down on, or laughed at. I became a prisoner in my own thoughts and I don't recommend this to anyone.

Then the battle inside my head just became too much for me to handle and I needed a confidant to get it all out too. Now I had gone to therapists but held back even with them in fear of judgement and shame. I am blessed that I have the best wife around who I had held at arm's length for most of our marriage, but sat on the couch with me as I poured everything out. I mean everything, and then she lovingly looked in my eyes and said, "See I'm still here!" That is when my life changed. I got it out. I released it and gained my power back and our relationship has blossomed even more since then! I have her to tell everything to and it's amazing.

I highly recommend you finding someone to trust and have as a confidant as this is when you will start to unleash your potential because it won't be stifled by fear.

SETTING THE PROPER COURSE

"Everybody has a plan until you get punched in the nose" is a famous quote by Mike Tyson, and I agree with him to a point. I have never boxed, but I have been popped in the nose accidentally so I can relate to how that changes everything! The pain is intense, your eyes are watering, and you are dazed and confused for a moment. How you thought you would handle yourself goes out the window quickly, but those who had a plan and prepared for a pop in the nose can quickly get back to their prepared game plan. If I was a boxer, I would 100% prepare and plan for a punch in the nose. If I'm going into a fight with another human, what do I think is going to happen? I know I will either effectively dodge the fist of my opponent or I will get hit. Have a plan on what to do next if you are able to dodge a blow, and have a plan for when you get hit. This is no different in how we should approach our life personally and professionally.

There needs to be a goal, a strategy, and the tactics necessary to get the work done. The fighter has a goal to win their fight, hopefully by a knockout, but they are fine with a win. Each fighter and trainer have different ideas of strategies they need to have to accomplish their goal. Some look at a fight and will even adjust their normal strategy based on the opponent. You may have a strategy to avoid the opponent to get them frustrated and exhausted, and another may be to go in swinging to catch the opponent off guard. Once the strategy has been established, now the tactics specific to the strategy are decided upon. Will there be a lot of body shots, uppercuts, dancing, and clinching? It all depends, and without knowing the strategy you cannot effectively plan the tactics. I hope this articulates the importance of establishing all three. You need a goal, strategy, and tactics to have a good plan.

I learned this concept when I transitioned from a field sales role and into marketing. One of my previous supervisors made a massive impact on my career by taking the time to help me understand the differences. This goes back to the importance of a mentor. As a career sales guy, I was focused on what I could do to convert the sale- the tactic.

Tactics are important, but you cannot establish a successful brand plan on a goal and tactics alone. The plan will be all over the place with no focus or direction. How many times are you making your plans with a goal and then a bunch of scattered tactics? I did it all the time!

The Oxford Dictionary defines a goal as the object of a person's ambition or effort; an aim or desired result. A "goal" by definition is simple, but there are many different opinions on how to set one. I believe the goal is the foundation of setting a proper course.

Strategy is defined as a plan of action or policy designed to achieve a major or objective. This is a critical step often overlooked, because if you're like me, I didn't know to think this way.

Tactic is defined as an action or strategy carefully planned to achieve a specific end. The key to this is specificity. This is what you will do to accomplish your goal based on the strategy. This is the action!

Think of these three like a pyramid.

We build everything about your plan off your goal. The goal is your foundation. Once you have the goal it is necessary to establish the strategy(s) you think will allow you to accomplish your goal. Finally, the tactics you will have to put into action based on the strategy to accomplish the goal.

Setting the Goal

A goal is the foundation to everything we do in life, and that is why I have it at the bottom of the pyramid. It sets everything in motion, and the lack of a well-defined goal is leaving too much to chance- unless leaving everything to chance is your goal. Crazy, I know, but it can be.

There have been so many unique books, podcasts, speakers, courses, coaches sharing their rules and thoughts for setting goals and one most will agree upon is a SMART goal. A SMART goal is Specific, Measurable, Attainable, Realistic, and Time bound. I agree with this almost 100% of the time, just not for a *big* goal.

What do I mean by *big* goal? A *big* goal to me is one that sets the course of your life or large life event. It is the course you will stay on because there is no finish line and only a current heading you into the sunset. I'll share what I mean by telling you my *big* goal. I went through a rough patch in my life not too long ago requiring me to get my act together. I had to make big changes that called for more than a SMART Goal. This required a goal that would change my life. The *big* goal I landed on was "to become the man God wants me to be." This is a goal that drives my actions every day. It is a goal that I can never accomplish, but by striving to meet that goal, I will become a better human, husband, father, son, brother, and friend. This is what I mean by a *big* goal.

Another example of a goal many can relate to is losing weight. In my experience, most people establish a SMART goal for losing weight, but SMART goals can limit our thinking. It may let us off the hook of really making a significant change, and it may limit further development and growth. Let's say I want to lose 15 pounds in six months. I set up a SMART goal and follow all the steps. It's specific, it's measurable, it's attainable, it's realistic, and time bound. I kick my butt into gear and restrict my calories by using a fitness app, increase my workouts by hiring a trainer, and track my weigh-ins. Six months later, I crossed the finish line victorious! I even lost five extra pounds! But, what's next? I may keep the weight off for several months, but since I was so restrictive to hit my goal or cross the finish line, I did not have a plan for after goal achievement. Thus, I go right back to my old ways. Now let's say you make a *big* goal for weight loss. Stop for a minute and think this through. What would a *big* goal for weight loss sound like? For me a *big* goal for weight loss would be to live a healthier lifestyle. This is a *big* goal that doesn't have a finish line, but it will drive daily decisions. I will use this example throughout the rest of this chapter to give you ideas on how you can make your own plan for success.

Establishing Strategies

Disclaimer: I am not a personal trainer or making recommendations on how to live a healthier life. I am just painting a picture so save the emails or the comments on ways to do it better.

Ok, you set your *big* goal to live a healthier lifestyle versus the smaller (but not less important) goal of losing 15 pounds in six months. You must remember not to forget this step of selecting strategies because this will get you organized on what tactics or "stuff" you need to take action on to live a healthier life.

I recommend not choosing over three strategies because any more than that will clutter your focus, but this plan isfor you to build to be helpful for how you operate. If you want five, knock yourself out.

When selecting strategies, you should think in the form of lanes or categories. For example, to live a healthier life you could focus on nutrition, physical fitness, and relaxation. These are three strategies that will lead you down a path to a healthier lifestyle. Without knowing the strategy to accomplish your goal, how would you even know what specific things you would need to do?

Assigning the Tactics

Your *big* goal is living a healthier lifestyle and your three key strategies are nutrition, physical fitness, and relaxation. Can you visualize this process of layering each part on top of each other? I have done this enough that I see it as a tree diagram. You could now start by drawing a box at the bottom of a piece of paper and write in "Live a Healthier lifestyle." Then draw three lines: one in the middle, and one on each corner going up to three individual boxes with your strategies written in each one. Then do the same from each strategy box, drawing three or more lines and at the end another box to write in your tactics.

The key to setting up tactics is to be specific. This is what you will do to accomplish your goal based on the strategy. Let's build this out as an example.

Strategy 1. Nutrition: you could eat more lean protein and vegetables five days per week, intermittent fasting three days per week, drink a gallon of water a day, and eliminate regular sodas.

Strategy 2. Physical fitness: increase brisk walking to 30 minutes, five days per week, go to trainer three days per week, and stretch for 30 minutes per day.

Strategy 3. Relaxation: 30 minutes of quiet time first thing in the morning, seven hours of sleep per night minimum, and no TV 1 hour before bed.

These strategies are very basic, and this is where you must be specific for where you are in whatever area you are focusing on. The beauty is once you have a *big* goal and the strategies, you more than likely won't ever have to change them. You will just alter the tactics as you improve and add variety.

Does all this make sense so far? There is no finish line to a *big* goal but a focal point to make a massive impact without feeling like you are saying "now what?" If everything is laid out properly you can just do those things repeatedly, and I guarantee you will live a healthier lifestyle.

Accountability

Building out a goal, strategy, and tactics are a lot of fun for me. I get excited and motivated writing everything out and thinking about how good I will feel accomplishing everything I have written on paper. I think big and get detailed on what I want to do; but now comes the part, if you are anything like me, that is the most difficult, and the part I routinely failed at. It is taking consistent action and seeing everything through to the end. This is because I didn't hold myself accountable to a scoreboard, and how often I would look at my progress or share my progress with others. This is accountability to yourself and the plan. Think about the last time you set out to accomplish something, even if you followed steps like what I just laid out above. Were you consistent in measuring your progress, and how often did you hold yourself accountable to check on your plan?

If you want to unleash your potential, you need to know how you are today versus yesterday so you can plan for tomorrow. It is an ongoing challenge that will last the rest of your life, and you will see the growth you didn't even know you were capable of.

What are some examples of holding yourself accountable or having a scoreboard to measure the progress towards the goal? Do not make this complicated and find what works best for you, but you must have something! I do different things based on the strategy and the tactics I am performing. Let's stick to the example we have already been using: living a healthier lifestyle and the strategy of nutrition.

Instead of just guessing on what you are eating and how often, there are apps or paper food journals to help you keep track of your nutrition. You can't just wing it because there is no accountability to doing the tactic you assigned to the strategy; if you don't measure it, you won't even know if it is working. This isn't any more difficult in professional or personal goals that have nothing to do with fitness or nutrition.

Be intentional in being accountable to the plan you have set. This won't happen by chance, and you will lose focus often along the way. You need to forgive yourself and get back on track. Don't give up because unleashing your potential is worth it.

CONCLUSION

What an amazing experience I have had writing this book. And you want to know what? I practice what I preached throughout this entire process. Nothing in this book is unique to me. It is not anything new. It is a compilation of trial and error and through the consumption of books, podcasts, videos, and coaching sessions throughout the course of my adult life. These learnings I am sharing have helped me recover when I fail, and I fail often. They have helped me get back on course after I lose sight of my goals or realize I never had the right ones set.

It is my hope that I have provided value to you, the reader, by sharing how I have been able to achieve more than I thought I ever could. I never thought I could write a book, and in less than 3 months at that. I never thought I could lose 85 pounds after high school and keep it off for 20 years. I never thought I could truly change my way of thinking from a negative, fixed-mindset to having a growth-mindset, looking for difficult and challenging things. I never thought I could reduce the anxiety that held me prisoner in my own head.

Four key steps I followed through the process:

1. Understanding yourself
2. Importance of communication
3. Developing yourself
4. Setting the proper course

Anyone and I mean anyone can follow these simple steps to unleashing their true potential. Stop being ordinary by sitting on the sidelines and not taking action. Be an active participant in your own future. Start writing your story today, but it won't happen by accident. I have separated myself from the crowd simply by being intentional about taking action.

The last thing I would like to share with you is my personal creed. Writing your own creed is incredibly powerful and helpful when you want to roll everything I have covered in this book into one place.

"I live a Christ-Like centered life focused on loving others. I am grateful for the abundance I have in every aspect of my life. I maintain a high level of integrity to live as a good example to others and keep promises I make to myself. I am confident in who I am and what I stand for."

I am blessed you took the time to read this book, and it's my hope I have added some value to you that will assist you in unleashing your potential.

"Don't worry about whether you're better than somebody else, but never cease trying to be the best you can become. You have control over that; the other you don't."

-John Wooden

ABOUT THE AUTHOR

Jeff Forrester has over 30 years of professional experience in retail, technology, and healthcare sales, training, marketing, and leadership. He has led multiple award-winning teams by leveraging his and the team's strengths and developing the weaknesses. He currently lives in Orlando, FL with his wife Tammy and two children Deuce and Lorelei.

To contact Jeff for coaching, speaking, or training you can reach him at 4activefutures@gmail.com or visit his website at www.active-futures.com.

NOTES

CPSIA information can be obtained
at www.ICGtesting.com
Printed in the USA
LVHW021504300720
661946LV00019B/710